The First Thanksgiving

CORNERSTONES OF FREEDOM™

SECOND SERIES

Andrew Santella

Children's Press®
A Division of Scholastic Inc.
New York • Toronto • London • Auckland • Sydney
Mexico City • New Delhi • Hong Kong
Danbury, Connecticut

Photographs © 2003: Art Resource, NY: cover bottom, 8 (Giraudon), 5 (Erich Lessing), 41 left (National Portrait Gallery, Smithsonian Institution); Bridgeman Art Library International Ltd., London/New York: 17 (City of Bristol Museum and Art Gallery, Avon, UK), 19 (Private Collection); Corbis Images: 7, 45 top right (Bettmann), 15 bottom (Owen Franken), 32 (Darrell Gulin), 33 bottom (Richard Hamilton Smith), 15 top (Angelo Hornak), 30 (Dave G. Houser), 28 (Wolfgang Kaehler), 26 (G.E. Kidder Smith), 44 right (Gunter Marx), 31 bottom, 45 bottom (Joe McDonald), 31 top (Greg Nikas), 29 (Roger Tidman), 33 top (Doug Wilson); Hulton|Archive/Getty Images: 11, 12 bottom, 23, 38, 39, 40 top, 45 top left; North Wind Picture Archives: 3, 12 top, 13, 14, 16, 18, 20, 21, 22, 34, 35, 37, 40 bottom, 44 left; Stock Montage, Inc.: cover top, 4, 25, 41 right; Viesti Collection, Inc./Alan Kearney: 9; Visuals Unlimited/R.F. Ashley: 36.

XNR Productions: Maps on 6, 7, 10, 44

Library of Congress Cataloging-in-Publication Data

Santella, Andrew.
   The First Thanksgiving/Andrew Santella
        p. cm. — (Cornerstones of freedom. Second series)
   Summary: Discusses the history of New Plymouth Colony in
Massachusetts, the relationship between the colonists and the native
Wampanoag people, and the harvest festival which would later become
Thanksgiving Day.
   Includes bibliographical references and index.
     ISBN 0-516-24204-0
     1. Thanksgiving Day—Juvenile literature. 2. Pilgrims (New Plymouth
Colony)—Social life and customs—Juvenile literature. 3. Massachu-
setts—History—New Plymouth, 1620–1691—Juvenile literature.
4. Massachusetts—Social life and customs—To 1775—Juvenile litera-
ture. [1. Thanksgiving Day. 2. Pilgrims (New Plymouth Colony)
3. Wampanoag Indians. 4. Indians of North America—Massachusetts.
5. Holidays. 6. Massachusetts—History—New Plymouth, 1620–1691.]
I. Title. II. Series.
   E162.S24 2003
   394.2649—dc21
                                    2002009031

1 2 3 4 5 6 7 8 9 10 R 12 11 10 09 08 07 06 05 04 03

I T HAD BEEN A TERRIBLE year of **hardship.** Disease and bitter cold had killed about half of the 102 people of the Plymouth colony. The others must have wondered if they had any hope of survival.

★　★　★　★

Then came the harvest of 1621. The colonists gathered more wheat, barley, and corn than they had even dared hope for. For the first time, it seemed possible that the colony would survive after all.

Survival would not have been possible without the help of the native people who had lived on the land for centuries. So it was only fitting that the Wampanoag people joined the colonists in celebrating the **lifesaving** harvest. The celebration has lived on in history as the first Thanksgiving. The colonists themselves did not call the celebration a thanksgiving feast, but without a doubt, the people of Plymouth had reason to be thankful. They would continue to thrive in their new home long after their harvest celebration, but for the Wampanoag, the future would prove less peaceful and less promising.

The English village of Scrooby was the original meeting place of the religious dissenters known as the Pilgrims.

THE SEARCH FOR RELIGIOUS FREEDOM

The colony at Plymouth had its beginnings in the religious conflicts of Europe in the early 1600s. We know the founders of Plymouth as the Pilgrims, but in their time they were known as Separatists. They were called Separatists because they had formed their own independent church. They believed that only by separating from the Church of England could they achieve a pure and honest religious faith. In 1606 they began meeting in Scrooby, a small town in Nottinghamshire, England.

Starting an independent church placed the Separatists in great danger in England. The Church of England was the country's official religion. Both the church and the country were led by the same person—King James I of England. To break away from the Church of England was to break away from England itself. To many in England, the Separatists were no better than **traitors** against their own king and country.

King James I of England took the throne in 1603. At the time, he had been king of Scotland for 36 years.

James I and his government saw the Separatists as troublemakers and kept a close watch on them. Government officials spied on the group's meetings. Not surprisingly, the Separatists began to fear that they might be jailed, or even

5

killed, for their religious beliefs. To avoid trouble with the government, the little community of believers moved from place to place. They met in several different English towns before realizing that their only hope was to look for a new home in another country. They decided to move to Holland, where the government allowed different forms of religious worship.

The Separatists found religious freedom in Holland, but still they faced problems. As immigrants in a foreign land, they struggled to **adapt** to new customs, a strange language, and unfamiliar ways of life. They also found that the only jobs available to immigrants in Holland were jobs that paid

The Separatists moved to Holland in search of religious freedom.

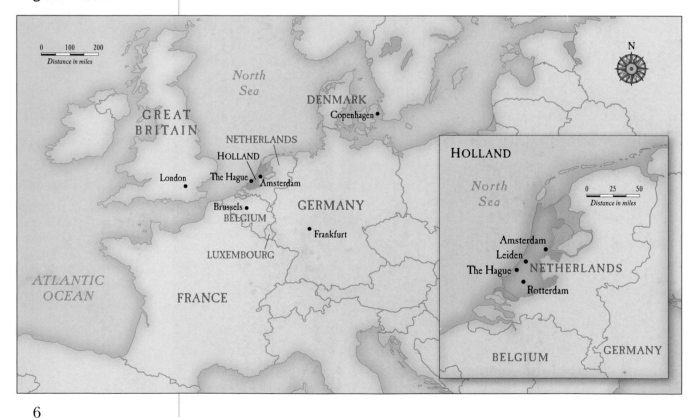

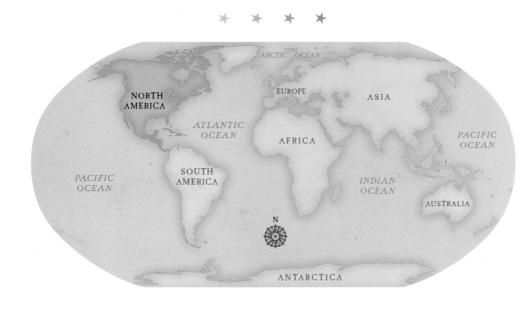

After finding more problems in Holland, the Separatists crossed the Atlantic Ocean to North America.

poorly and required hard labor. After twelve years in Holland the community of Separatists decided to move again. This time, they would cross the ocean to build a new home on the shores of North America.

MAYFLOWER II

A full-scale **reproduction** of the *Mayflower* is docked at the Plimoth Plantation museum in Massachusetts. The *Mayflower II* was built with the same materials, such as English oak and hemp rope, that would have been available to the original colonists. The ship was completed in 1957 and sailed from England to Plymouth that year.

The *Mayflower* passengers first came ashore in the New World in November 1602. Only 37 of the 102 colonists were actually Separatists.

FOUNDING PLYMOUTH

To pay for their ocean voyage to North America, the Separatists turned to a group of English merchants. The merchants agreed to pay for the voyage and to set up a colony in North America. In return, the colonists agreed to work at farming and fishing to make the colony a success and to earn a profit. After seven years the merchants and the colonists would divide up the profits and the property.

The merchants also recruited more people to increase the size of the colony and ensure its success. The Separatists called these new recruits "strangers" because they were not members of their religious congregation. On July 21, 1620, the Separatists sailed from Leiden, Holland, to Southampton, England, aboard the ship *Speedwell*. Before leaving, they held a long prayer service. One of their leaders, William Bradford, later wrote, "So they left that goodly and pleasant city which had been their resting place twelve years; but they knew they were pilgrims."

In Southampton, the Leiden Separatists planned to meet up with the other colonists and a larger ship called the *Mayflower*. However, they were delayed by problems with the *Speedwell*. The little ship leaked badly and needed repairs. Each time they tried to repair the ship, another problem would appear. Finally, they decided to leave the troublesome *Speedwell* behind in Southampton. Separatist and stranger alike would sail for North America aboard the *Mayflower*.

Before transporting the Plymouth colonists in 1620, the *Mayflower* had been used by merchants and traders. Among other things, the ship had carried lumber, fish, and wine. It was probably about 113 feet (34.4 meters) long and 25 feet (7.6 m) wide. Now 102 passengers and about 30 crew members squeezed onto the ship. Their journey lasted sixty-six long days. The *Mayflower* sailed through storms and rough water. Many of the passengers were seasick. All were wet and miserable.

The *Mayflower* had been used to transport lumber and other goods.

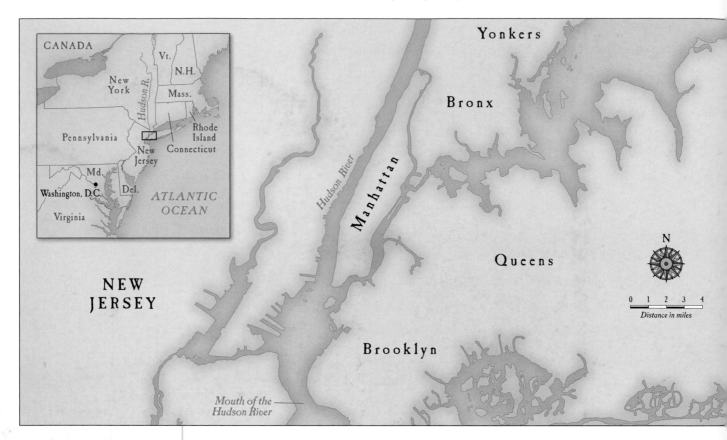

The Pilgrims intended to land near the mouth of the Hudson River, in present-day New York.

One passenger died on the Mayflower crossing, and one child was born—a boy named Oceanus Hopkins. Life on board ships in the 1600s was difficult. Passengers lived on supplies of food that could spoil quickly. Because the ocean contains salt water, which they could not drink, travelers depended on supplies of fresh water stored in casks. After a few weeks at sea, the water might be covered by a film of scum.

Plymouth's founders wanted plenty of room for their new colony, and they wanted no more interference from outsiders. So they decided to settle as far away as possible from other English people in North America. They intended to settle the area around the mouth of the Hudson River, at the very northern edge of what was then known as Virginia. Today, New York City stands there. However, the Pilgrims did not land where they had intended to land.

Instead, after their long and dangerous journey the Pilgrims found themselves off the coast of Cape Cod in Massachusetts. They made their first landing in North America at present-day Provincetown, at the tip of Cape Cod, in November 1620. They were about 200 miles (322 kilometers) northeast of their intended destination, but they had had enough of ocean travel. They had spent more than two months packed onto a small, uncomfortable ship, tossed about by choppy ocean waters. They were ready to live on land again, even if it was not the land they had sailed for. The Pilgrims would make their new home in Massachusetts.

Miles Standish was hired by the Pilgrims to be their military leader.

First, a group of sixteen colonists led by Miles Standish searched for a place on the rocky coastline to build their new colony. They found a supply of corn, some beads and ornaments, and a few baskets and kettles left behind by some native people. Standish and his group took whatever they found. One colonist wrote, "And sure it was God's

The founder of the Jamestown colony in Virginia in 1607, Captain John Smith also explored parts of New England.

good providence that we found this corn, for else we know not how we should have done." To the native people, however, it probably seemed that the colonists were simply thieves.

In a small boat, the colonists explored the coastline for a month. Finally, a storm blew them into a harbor southwest of Provincetown on the Massachusetts mainland. Earlier, English explorer John Smith had named the place New Plymouth, after a town in England. To the Pilgrims, it looked like a good place to start their colony. What the Pilgrims liked best about the spot was that someone had already cleared fields for planting crops. That meant they would not have to do the hard work of chopping down

Standish and settlers follow a Native American scout.

With winter already upon them, the Pilgrims worked quickly to build new homes at Plymouth.

trees, digging out tree stumps, and removing rocks and boulders. (According to legend, the colonists went ashore at Plymouth Rock. But there is no evidence that this really happened.) In late December of 1620 the Pilgrims got to work building their new homes. In their rush to get settled, they were almost too busy to wonder about the mysteries of Plymouth: Who had cleared the fields, why did they no longer live there, and what had happened to them?

Forty-one of the colonists signed the Mayflower Compact.

THE MAYFLOWER COMPACT

Before the colonists went ashore at Plymouth, their leaders drew up a document for the head of every household to sign. The signers pledged loyalty to the king of England and agreed to go along with the wishes of the community. Known as the Mayflower Compact, it was the first written document to establish a foundation for government in what is now the United States.

THE WAMPANOAG

The colonists did not know it, but they were building their new settlement on the exact site of a Wampanoag village. It was one of many Wampanoag villages spread across what is now Massachusetts and Rhode Island. The Wampanoag called the village Patuxet, and they had farmed and fished there for centuries. They lived in bark-covered wigwams called *wetus*. Each Wampanoag family farmed its own plot of land, where they planted corn, beans, squash, and even watermelon. The Wampanoag often spent spring and summer

Wampanoag dwellings were known as *wetus*. This is an example of a smaller type, known as a *puhuckakuan.*

along the ocean's shores, farming and gathering cod, herring, mussels, and clams. They gathered for large community hunts in late autumn and early winter, then moved inland for the rest of the winter.

This way of life was disrupted by the arrival of Europeans in Wampanoag country around 1600. Fishermen, traders, and explorers from England, Holland, and France began sailing up and down the coast of New England, making contact with the native people. These first encounters

Wampanoag means "people of the first light," or "eastern people," in the Wampanoag language.

Littleneck clams were a major part of the Wampanoag diet.

15

were not always peaceful. Some traders captured native people, took them to islands in the Caribbean Sea, and sold them into slavery. In 1614 an English captain named Thomas Hunt captured twenty Wampanoag from Patuxet village and seven more from Nauset village and attempted to sell them into slavery in Spain.

Colonists barter with Native Americans for furs. The fur trade was a major stimulus to the European settlement of North America.

16

Fishing boats from Bristol Harbor visited North America as early as the late fifteenth century.

One of the captured Wampanoag was Tisquantum, or Squanto, as he is sometimes called. He lived for a time with a group of Spanish **friars,** then made his way to Bristol in England. Bristol was a major seaport, and the sailors there were very interested in Tisquantum's knowledge of New England and its native people. Before long, Tisquantum was sailing back to North America, this time as a guide for a voyage of exploration. Working with English captain Thomas Dermer, Tisquantum made his way back to his home village of Patuxet in 1619.

It should have been a joyous homecoming for the long-lost Tisquantum. There was only one problem. His people had vanished. In 1618 a terrible wave of disease had swept

An epidemic killed the Wamapanoag people of Patuxet. Disease was the greatest threat to native peoples in contact with whites.

over the Wampanoag country, passing from village to village. Its effects were devastating. Patuxet was entirely wiped out. Tisquantum was the sole survivor of his village, and he was only alive because he had been away when the **epidemic** arrived.

Historians are not certain what disease struck New England in 1618. It may have been smallpox, a highly contagious disease that can cause disfigurement and death. It was no coincidence that the wave of disease arrived at the same time the European explorers and traders arrived. The Europeans brought diseases with them that were entirely new to the native people and to which the native people had no **immunity**, or resistance. Over the next several

★ ★ ★ ★

hundred years many groups of native people across North America were completely wiped out by smallpox and other diseases brought by Europeans. The epidemic that destroyed Patuxet in 1618 changed everything for the Wampanoag. Villages that were not wiped out were severely weakened. The population of the Wampanoag people drastically declined. Neighboring peoples took advantage of the weakness of the Wampanoag and began invading their territory. The Narragansett made the Wampanoag pay them a **tribute**—a kind of forced payment made in exchange for peace and protection.

It was the epidemic of 1618 that left the fields of Patuxet deserted for the Plymouth colonists. It was the epidemic that also left the Wampanoag so weakened that they had little choice but to seek peace with the colonists.

THE LANGUAGE OF THE WAMPANOAG

The Wampanoag language is a complex one called Wôpanâak. Some Wampanoag words have become part of the English language. The English word "succotash," a dish made from corn and beans, comes from the Wampanoag word "sukahtash."

Unlike the Wampanoag, the more powerful Narragansetts had no desire to make peace with the English newcomers to their territory.

A FIRST ENCOUNTER

For the first few months at their new home, the people of Plymouth had no direct contact with the native people of the area. That changed on March 16, 1621. That day, a lone figure walked confidently into the little settlement and proclaimed in English, "Welcome, Englishmen!" The man's name was Samoset, and he was a leader of the Abenaki people. Samoset and the Abenaki lived along the coast of what is now Maine, but in the spring of 1621 he was visiting the Wampanoag in Massachusetts. He had learned to speak a bit of English from the fishermen who were already making frequent stops along the coast of Maine. He carried two arrows with him—one sharpened at its tip, the other blunt. Perhaps the two arrows were a

The colonist Edward Winslow described Samoset's arrival at Plymouth: "He came all alone and along the houses to the rendezvous, where we intercepted him."

Tisquantum greets the Pilgrims. Although he had twice been taken captive by the English, Tisquantum welcomed the Plymouth colonists.

message to the colonists that the natives were ready for either war or peace.

The people of Plymouth were amazed to find this English-speaking Native American suddenly in their midst. They spent hours asking him questions about their new home. It was from Samoset that the colonists finally learned the fate of the people of Patuxet. Samoset also told them that nearby was another Wampanoag village of about three hundred people called Nemasket, and that the great Wampanoag sachem, or leader, Massasoit could be found there. As Samoset and the colonists talked on and on, the colonists fed Samoset and supplied him with a coat to ward off the cold. That night, Samoset stayed in Plymouth. One

The colonists who met Massasoit in March 1621 were very impressed by the Wampanoag sachem. They described him as "spare of speech" and "courageous," wearing a black wolf skin on his shoulder and with his face painted red.

of the colonists described him: "He was a man free in speech, so far as he could express his mind, and of a seemly carriage . . . He was a tall, straight man, the hair of his head black, long behind, only short before, none on his face at all."

His first meeting with the colonists went so well that he returned after a few days. This time, he brought with him Tisquantum. After his years spent as a prisoner and guide to the English, Tisquantum spoke better English than Samoset. The conversation between native people and

newcomers flowed freely. Tisquantum told the people of Plymouth that his sachem, Massasoit, wanted to meet them. Indeed, later that day Massasoit and sixty other Wampanoag appeared outside the village. Their arrival must have created some concern among the people of Plymouth, but their governor, John Carver, sent some representatives to meet with Massasoit. With Tisquantum acting as translator, the colonists and the Wampanoag reached a peace agreement. It called for the Wampanoag and the Plymouth colonists to come to one another's aid.

Not long after the peace agreement, Carver died and was succeeded as governor by William Bradford. Later, Bradford recalled the terms of the treaty with Massasoit: "If any did unjustly war against him, we would aid him; if any did war against us, he should aid us." The treaty also called for both sides to leave their weapons at home when they visited each other: "That when their men came to us, they should leave their bows and arrows behind them, as we should do our pieces [guns] when we came to them." The agreement benefited both sides. With their steel tools and their firearms, the colonists made a powerful ally for the Wampanoag in

William Bradford was the governor of the Plymouth colony. His wife drowned when she fell off the *Mayflower* while it was still anchored at Provincetown.

★ ★ ★ ★

their conflicts with other native peoples. For their part, the Wampanoag would offer the knowledge and protection that would help the Plymouth colony survive.

Later that year, Bradford sent Massasoit a chain made of copper. He sent word that any of Massosoit's people who came to Plymouth carrying the chain would be welcomed as a special guest. As a sign of goodwill, Massasoit asked a trusted adviser named Hobbamock to live with the colonists at Plymouth. Most likely, Massasoit also wanted Hobbamock to keep an eye on the colonists and report on their activities. The colonists came to trust Hobbamock, calling him their "friend and interpreter." Hobbamock and his family were the only Wampanoag to live in Plymouth during the 1620s. Hobbamock was a *pniese,* or warrior-counselor. One colonial writer defined the pniese as "men of great courage and wisdom."

Hobbamock's house, or *wetu,* was probably made of bent cedar poles covered by sheets of bark. A typical Wampanoag wetu was about 20 feet (6.1 m) long and 12 feet (3.7 m) wide. An English visitor to the area in 1620 described the typical Wampanoag house: "The houses were made with long yong [young] Sapling trees, bended and both ends stucke in the ground; they were made round . . . and covered downe to the ground with thicke and well wrought matts, and the doore was not over a yard high, made of a matt to open; the chimney was a wide open hole in the top, for which they had a matt to cover it close when they please."

PLANTING THE FIRST CROP

Building the Plymouth Colony

On April 5, 1621, the *Mayflower* left Plymouth for England with its crew of sailors. The fifty-two surviving colonists stayed on, ready to build their new colony after their terrible

Reconstructed seventeenth-century Pilgrim houses. The reconstructed houses use shingled roofs instead of straw roofs like the colonists, but otherwise are very similar.

winter of suffering. They were not on their own, however. That spring, their Wampanoag neighbors looked after the newcomers. Hobbamock and Tisquantum gave the colonists advice on planting crops, hunting, and other activities important to their survival. In Plymouth the colonists slowly grew healthier and stronger as the weather improved. They continued to build their new settlement. By summer, they completed a meetinghouse, two storehouses for food and supplies, and seven dwelling houses. They also completed a cannon platform on a hilltop overlooking the settlement. Plymouth was starting to look like a small village.

The colonists' houses at Plymouth were constructed quickly and were not fancy. They were probably one-story tall and made of oak or other hardwoods. Their roofs were thatched with reeds or straw, and their floors were hardened dirt. The colonists used no nails to build their houses. The timbers that made up the houses were cut to fit together at the joints, one timber fitting into a slot cut into another timber.

The colonists kept busy that spring planting their first crops in their new land. The advice of Tisquantum and other Wampanoag about planting proved extremely valuable. Over the centuries, the Wampanoag had developed highly successful methods for farming the rocky soil of New England. They had learned to use carefully constructed fires to clear away trees and other plant growth from fields. This allowed them to prepare soil for planting using only stone, shell, and wood tools. Native traditions called for planting to begin in late April, or when the budding leaves of dogwood trees became the size of a squirrel's ear.

★　★　★　★

The Wampanoag soaked corn kernels in water overnight before planting them. The corn was planted in rows, three or four inches deep. Once the new corn had grown a few inches, they planted beans alongside. The growing bean vines could then climb up the cornstalks, using them for support.

LEARNING FROM THE WAMPANOAG

Tisquantum taught the Plymouth colonists to enrich the soil by using the abundant fish of the area as a **fertilizer.** He had the colonists bury the fish in the crop fields so that as the fish decayed, they would feed **nutrients** back into the soil. Tisquantum warned the colonists that if they didn't use fish as a fertilizer, their crops "would come to nothing." The

Europeans were used to eating herring, but Tisquantum showed them how to use the fish as fertilizer as well.

As the colonists were soon to learn, birds such as the common grackle love to feed on corn.

colonists heeded Tisquantum's advice. Later, a colonist named Edward Winslow wrote to a friend back in England: "[W]e set last spring some twenty acres of Indian corn and sowed some six acres of barley and peas. According to the manner of the Indians, we manured our ground with herrings which we have in great abundance and take with great ease at our doors."

After the fish had been placed in the fields, farmers had to keep watch over the fields to make sure that wolves and other animals didn't dig up the fish and eat them. This could not have been pleasant duty, with the smell of rotting fish in the air.

About a month after planting, the fields were weeded again and dirt was mounded around the cornstalks so they would not blow over easily. Then, the crops were left alone until harvest time. They still had to be watched, though.

Cornmeal was used by the
Pilgrims for making breads
and cakes.

Blackbirds and crows could eat away most of a season's corn crop. The Wampanoag built watch houses in the fields, where women and children stayed to scare off animals that came near the plants. By late July or early August, green beans and summer squash were ready to be picked. Green, or unripe, corn could be picked in September, but mature corn was not ready until early October. The Wampanoag taught the colonists to boil some of the corn, then dry it on mats in the sun, and store it in baskets for future use. The rest of the corn could be cooked as kernels or ground into cornmeal for making breads and cakes.

In all, the colonists planted about 20 acres (8.1 hectares) of corn, plus 6 acres (2.4 ha) of barley and wheat. These crops were not their only source of food, of course. They found the woods around Plymouth full of deer, bear, and turkey. The rivers and brooks were teeming with eels and fish. With the Wamapanoag peace agreement in place, the colonists felt safe enough to venture deep into the forested countryside to hunt and fish. They were turning Plymouth into a productive new home.

Wild turkey and white-tailed deer were found in large numbers in the woods around Plymouth.

31

Wheat (above), barley (far right), and corn (lower right) were part of the bountiful harvests the Plymouth colonists celebrated in the autumn of 1621.

CELEBRATING THE HARVEST

After a year of hardship, the people of Plymouth colony finally had reason to celebrate. It was autumn of 1621, and they were gathering the crops they had planted in the spring of that year. When they had planted the crops, the colonists had little cause to believe that their tiny new settlement would survive for very long. They were far from home, in a strange land that seemed to be a place of death. Disease and bitter cold had taken their toll on the colony. At one point in that terrible first year, only seven of the colonists were healthy enough to take care of the dozens of weak and sick. About half of the 102 original colonists died. The Plymouth colony had nearly been wiped out in its first year.

The harvest of 1621 gave the people of Plymouth hope that they would make it. The colonists were amazed at the bounty. Wampanoag farming methods helped them produce a wonderful harvest. The crops they gathered in the fall would help them survive their second winter at Plymouth.

With their first harvest in, and having survived nearly a year in their new home, the colonists began planning a celebration. Although this celebration has come to be called the first Thanksgiving, the colonists would never have given it such a name. To them a feast of thanksgiving would

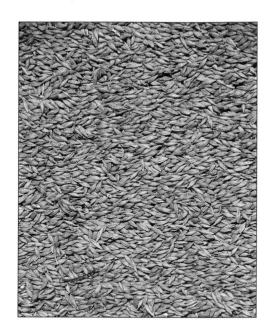

Massasoit's friendliness toward the colonists made him a welcome guest at their harvest feast.

have been a religious event. The celebration that went on in the autumn of 1621 was based on harvest celebrations they remembered from their days in England. It included activities that would have never been part of the colonists' religious events. With three days of dancing and games and large quantities of food, what we call the first Thanksgiving was really a grand party. Colonist Edward Winslow described it: "Our harvest being gotten in, our governor sent four men on fowling [hunting for fowl, or wild birds], that so we might after a special manner rejoice together after we had gathered the fruits of our labors. They four in one day killed as much fowl as . . . served the company almost a week."

The nearby Wampanoag probably heard the shooting of the hunting party and went to investigate. Massasoit arrived at Plymouth with ninety men. When they learned that the colonists were planning a celebration, the Wampanoag joined in. Massasoit sent out hunters of his own. "They went out and killed five [deer], which they brought to the plantation and bestowed on our governor, and upon the captain and others," Winslow reported.

For three days the fifty-two colonists and ninety Wampanoag "entertained and feasted." All we know for

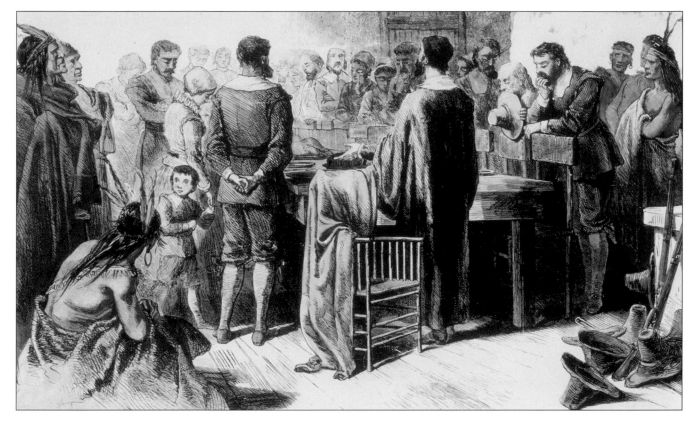

The actual first Thanksgiving feast differed from this artist's portrayal in at least one significant way: It probably took place outdoors.

sure of the feast comes from two brief eyewitness accounts, one written by Winslow and the other by Bradford. Winslow's account of the feast mentions two foods: the wild fowl that Bradford's hunters supplied and the five deer that Massasoit and his hunters brought. Over the years, the turkey dinner has become an important part of the legend of the first Thanksgiving. But, in fact, there is no evidence that the colonists and Wampanoag ate turkey at their feast. Winslow only mentions "wild fowl," which includes turkey, duck, and other birds. Most likely, there was also cod, shellfish, rabbit, squash, beans, and other **delicacies.** For dessert the colonists might have enjoyed nuts and fruit. Without a doubt, sweet potatoes were not served, because they were not yet grown in New England. No cranberry sauce was served either. Cranberries were available, but not the sugar needed to make a sauce.

Most of the feasting must have taken place outdoors because Plymouth did not yet have a building big enough to hold so many people. Most likely, Governor Bradford and other leaders of the colony ate at one table, where they were served the best food. Massasoit would have been treated as a special guest and shown great respect. He might have joined Plymouth's leaders at the "high table." There they enjoyed not just one large meal but several meals over the course of the three-day celebration.

DINING PLYMOUTH-STYLE

Dining customs at the Plymouth colony differed from today's customs. One of the biggest differences is that the colonists did not use forks. They did use knives and spoons, but mostly they just dug in with their hands.

Cranberries were available for the first Thanksgiving, but cranberry sauce was not made for the feast.

Preparing all those meals required a great deal of work. Corn had to be ground, birds plucked of their feathers, meat roasted, and shellfish gathered. Most likely, all of the colonists pitched in to help prepare the meal.

A BROKEN PEACE

The feast gave the Wampanoag and the people of Plymouth the chance to learn more about each other. They celebrated their friendship and the peace agreement between the two peoples. They competed in contests of skill and strength, races, wrestling matches, and long-jumping contests. The colonists probably watched wide-eyed while the Wampanoag performed traditional dances. Miles Standish and his small troop of fourteen soldiers put on a display of military drills. For those three days, it must have seemed possible that the

37

Settlers drive back a Pequot force in the Pequot War. The war ended with the complete destruction of the Pequot people.

WAMPANOAG THANKSGIVING

The Wampanoag had their own thanksgiving traditions. For centuries they had celebrated festivals such as the "Strawberry Thanksgiving" and the "Green Corn Thanksgiving" at different times of the year. Their celebrations included songs, dances, and stories that reminded them to give thanks for all they had been given. It was a tradition for Wampanoag families to share food with their neighbors during these festivals.

colonists and the Wampanoag could live together in harmony.

The promise of friendship between the Wampanoag and the colonists would not last. Plymouth kept growing. In fact, just days after the 1621 harvest celebration, a ship filled with new colonists landed at Plymouth. By 1627 the population of the colony was one hundred and fifty. Between 1630 and 1640, the colony grew from three hundred people to nearly two thousand. That rapid growth created an increased demand for land, which led to disputes between the colonists and the native people of the area. By 1637, natives and colonists were at war. That year, a military force from Plymouth and other colonies massacred a Pequot village. In 1675, Massasoit's son Metacomet attempted to unite the native people of New England in a war against the English. The war that followed came to be called King Philip's War, after the English name for Metacomet. The war was a disaster for the native people of New England. Metacomet was killed, his son was enslaved, and the Wampanoag lost their homeland.

A HOLIDAY TRADITION

It may be known as the first Thanksgiving, but the 1621 harvest celebration did not become a tradition right away. There was a Plymouth Thanksgiving in 1623, but this was a more religious event than the 1621 celebration. Also, it was not held in the fall, but in the middle of summer. It was held in gratitude for a rainfall that ended a two-month-long drought and saved the colony's crops. By the mid-

In explaining his decision to fight the English settlers, Metacomet said, "I am determined not to live until I have no country."

Sara Josepha Hale was one of the most important female editors and journalists of her day.

1600s it had become a tradition for the people of New England to celebrate annual days of thanksgiving.

However, the first national day of thanksgiving was not declared until 1777. That year, the Continental Congress proclaimed a holiday to give thanks for the victory over the British at the Battle of Saratoga. Interest in the history of the Plymouth colony grew in the 1840s, when historians rediscovered the letters and other documents of the colonists. Around that time, historians began incorrectly referring to the 1621 harvest celebration as the first Thanksgiving. In 1846, Sara Josepha Hale, editor of the popular magazine *Godey's Lady's Book,* began a **campaign** to make Thanksgiving a national holiday.

The modern Thanksgiving tradition was begun by Abraham Lincoln in 1863. That year, he declared two Thanksgiving days. One was held in August to celebrate the Union victory at Gettysburg in the Civil War. The other was held in

In 1777, a thanksgiving celebration was held to mark the colonists' victory at the Battle of Saratoga, a turning point in the American Revolution.

Presidents Abraham Lincoln (left) and Franklin D. Roosevelt (right) played important roles in making Thanksgiving a national holiday.

November to give thanks for the nation's blessings. The autumn celebration caught on and has been a tradition ever since. In 1941, President Franklin Roosevelt signed a bill establishing the fourth Thursday of every November as Thanksgiving Day. By then, Thanksgiving Day family gatherings and turkey dinners had become part of American life.

Today's Thanksgiving traditions bear only a slight resemblance to the original 1621 harvest celebration. However, many native people remember the feast at Plymouth in their own way. They gather each Thanksgiving at the statue of Massasoit that stands in Plymouth and observe the day in silence. It is their salute to the memory of the native people who welcomed and helped the people of Plymouth.

41

Glossary

adapt—to change or make adjustments to better thrive in a certain place or set of conditions

campaign—a series of activities for a special purpose to achieve a certain goal

delicacies—things that taste good or in other ways appeal to the senses

epidemic—an outbreak of disease among the population of a specific area

fertilizer—a material used to make the soil more productive

friars—members of certain religious orders in the Roman Catholic Church

hardship—a situation that is difficult to endure

immunity—the state of being protected from a disease

lifesaving—rescuing a person or people from death

nutrient—a substance that provides nourishment
   to a living thing

reproduction—a copy of an object or image

traitors—people who are disloyal to their country.

tribute—a payment made by one person or group of people
   to a more powerful person or group of people, under
   threat of punishment

Timeline: The First

1606	1608		1618	1620	1621	1627

1606
The Separatists, or Pilgrims, begin meeting in Scrooby, England.

1608

Map: North Sea, Amsterdam, Leiden, The Hague, NETHERLANDS, Rotterdam. 0 25 50 Distance in miles

The Pilgrims move to Leiden in Holland.

1618
Disease sweeps through native villages of Massachusetts, killing many.

1620
The Pilgrims cross the Atlantic on the *Mayflower* and establish colony at Plymouth.

1621
The colonists and Wampanoag neighbors celebrate the first harvest at Plymouth.

1627
The population of Plymouth grows to one hundred and fifty.

Thanksgiving

1637	1675	1846	1863	1941	1957

The English massacre Pequot villagers during the Pequot War.

Metacomet launches war against English colonists.

Sarah Josepha Hale begins campaign to make Thanksgiving a national holiday.

Abraham Lincoln declares national Day of Thanksgiving

Franklin Roosevelt signs a bill making the fourth Thursday of November Thanksgiving Day.

Mayflower II, a reproduction of the original ship, sails from England to Massachusetts.

To Find Out More

BOOKS

Collier, Christopher and James Lincoln Collier. *Pilgrims and Puritans, 1620-1676.* Tarrytown, NY: Benchmark Books, 1998.

Grace, Catherine O'Neill and Margaret M. Bruchac. *1621: A New Look at Thanksgiving.* Washington, D.C.: National Geographic Society, 2001.

ONLINE SITES

Plimoth Plantation Living Museum
http://www.plimoth.org

Pilgrim Hall Museum
http://www.pilgrimhall.org

Index

Bold numbers indicate illustrations.

About the Author

Andrew Santella writes for magazines and newspapers, including *Gentlemen's Quarterly* and the *New York Times Book Review*. He is the author of several Children's Press books, including *Daniel Boone and the Cumberland Gap*, *U.S. Presidential Inaugurations*, and *September 11, 2001* for Cornerstones of Freedom, Second Series.